THIS BOOK BELONGS TO

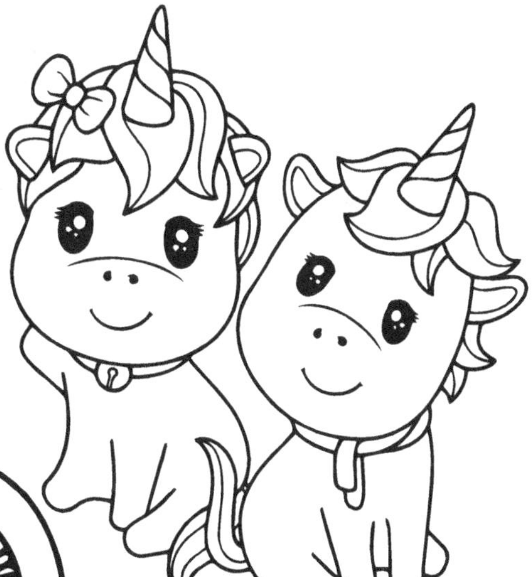

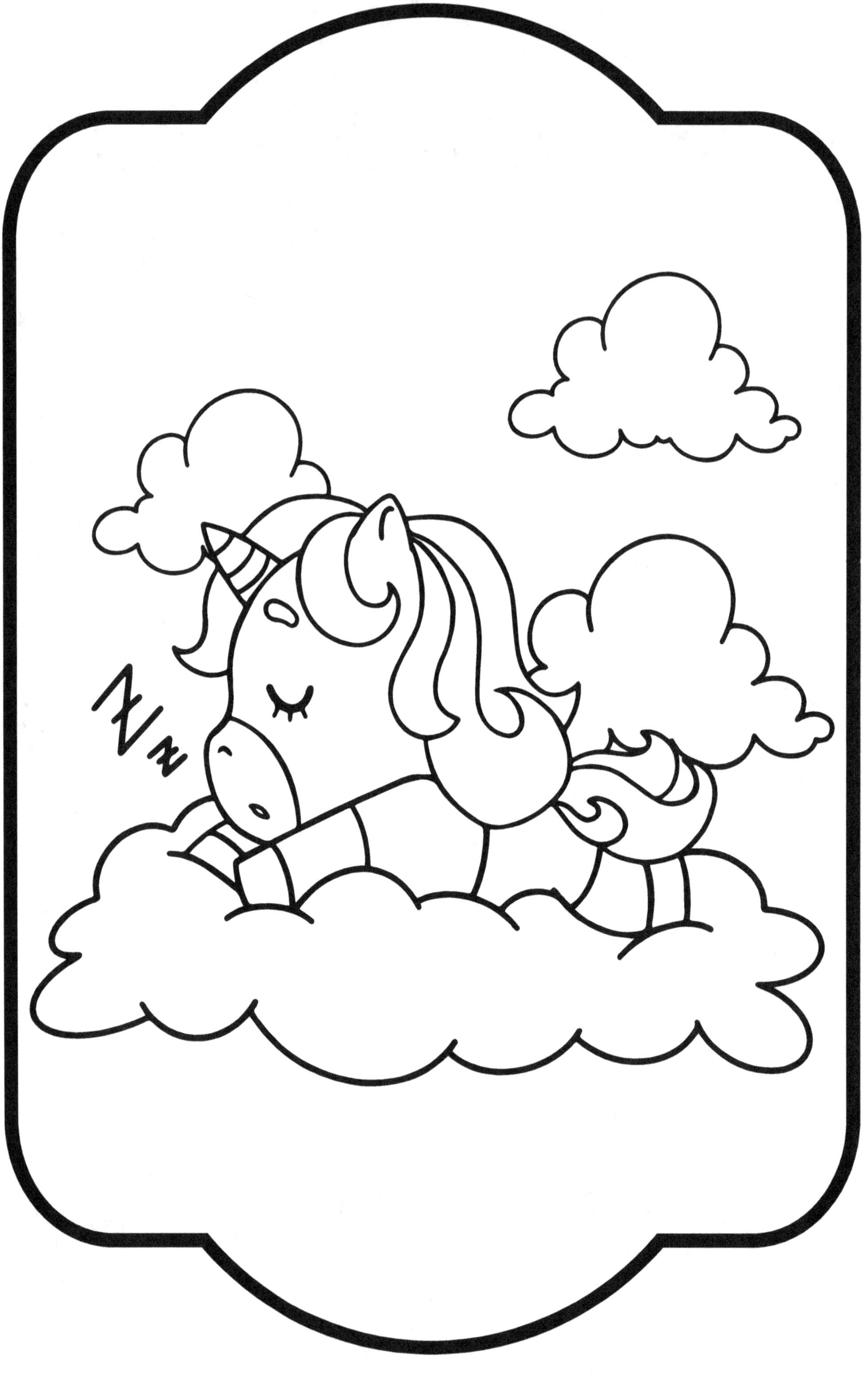

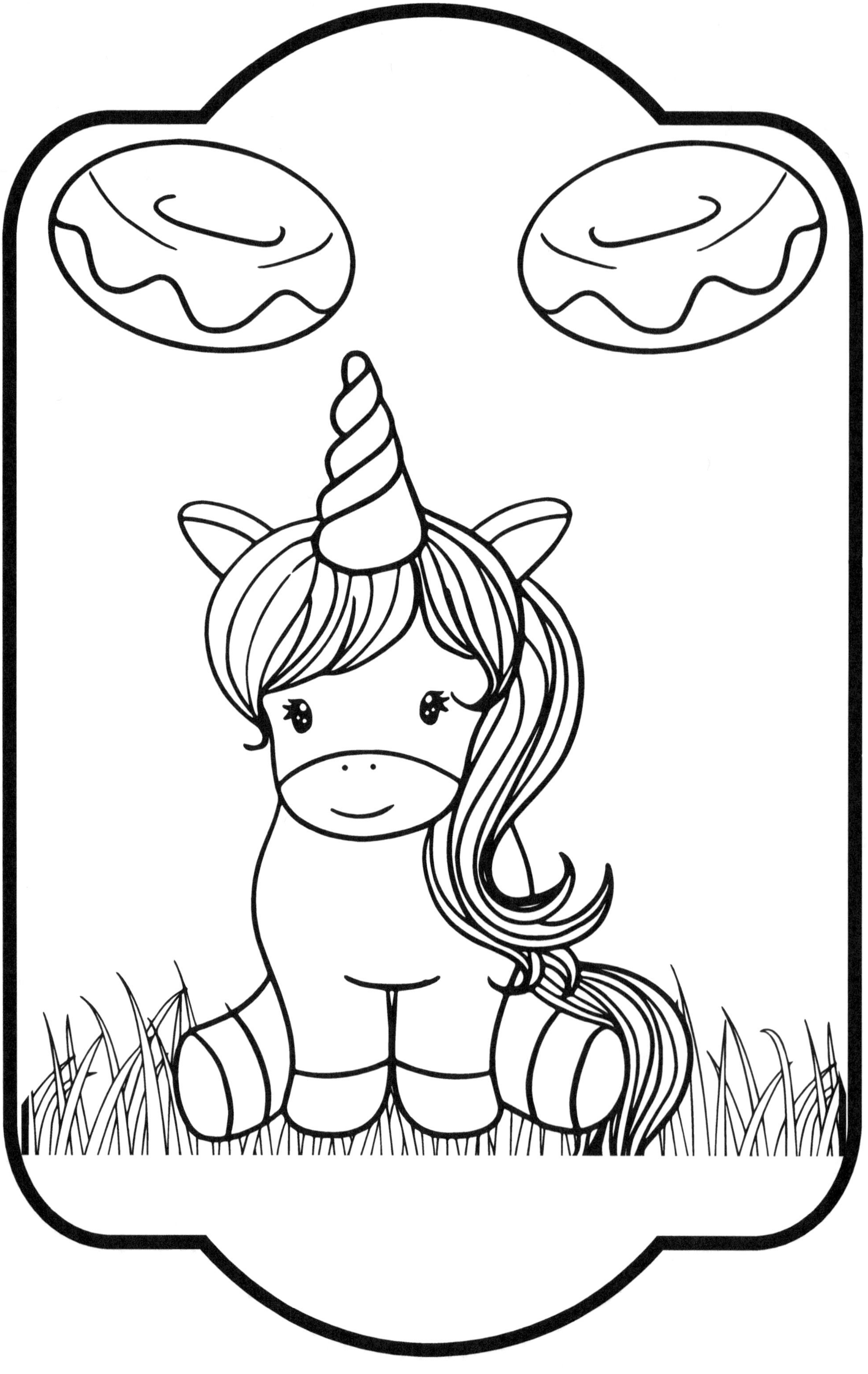

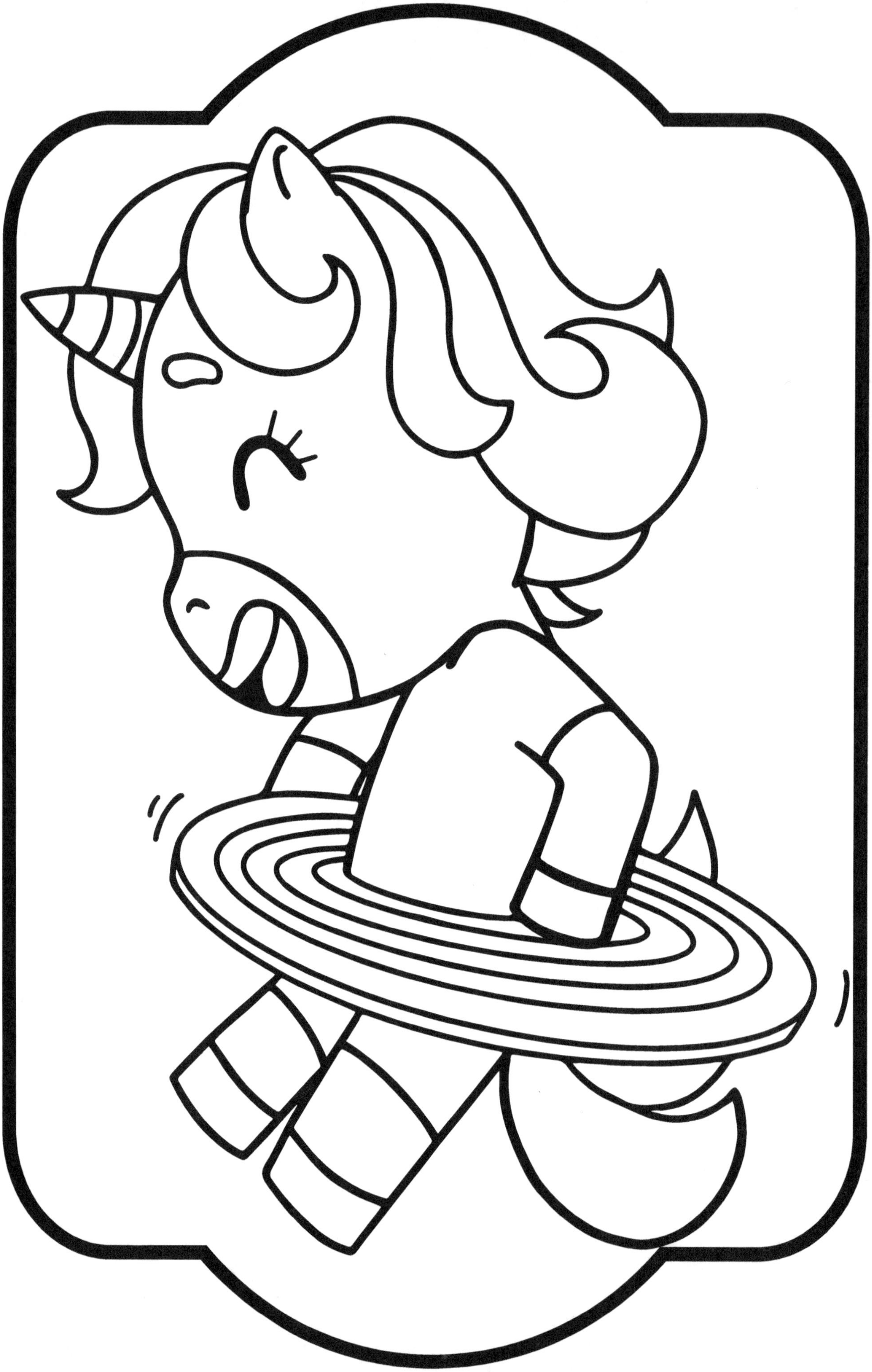

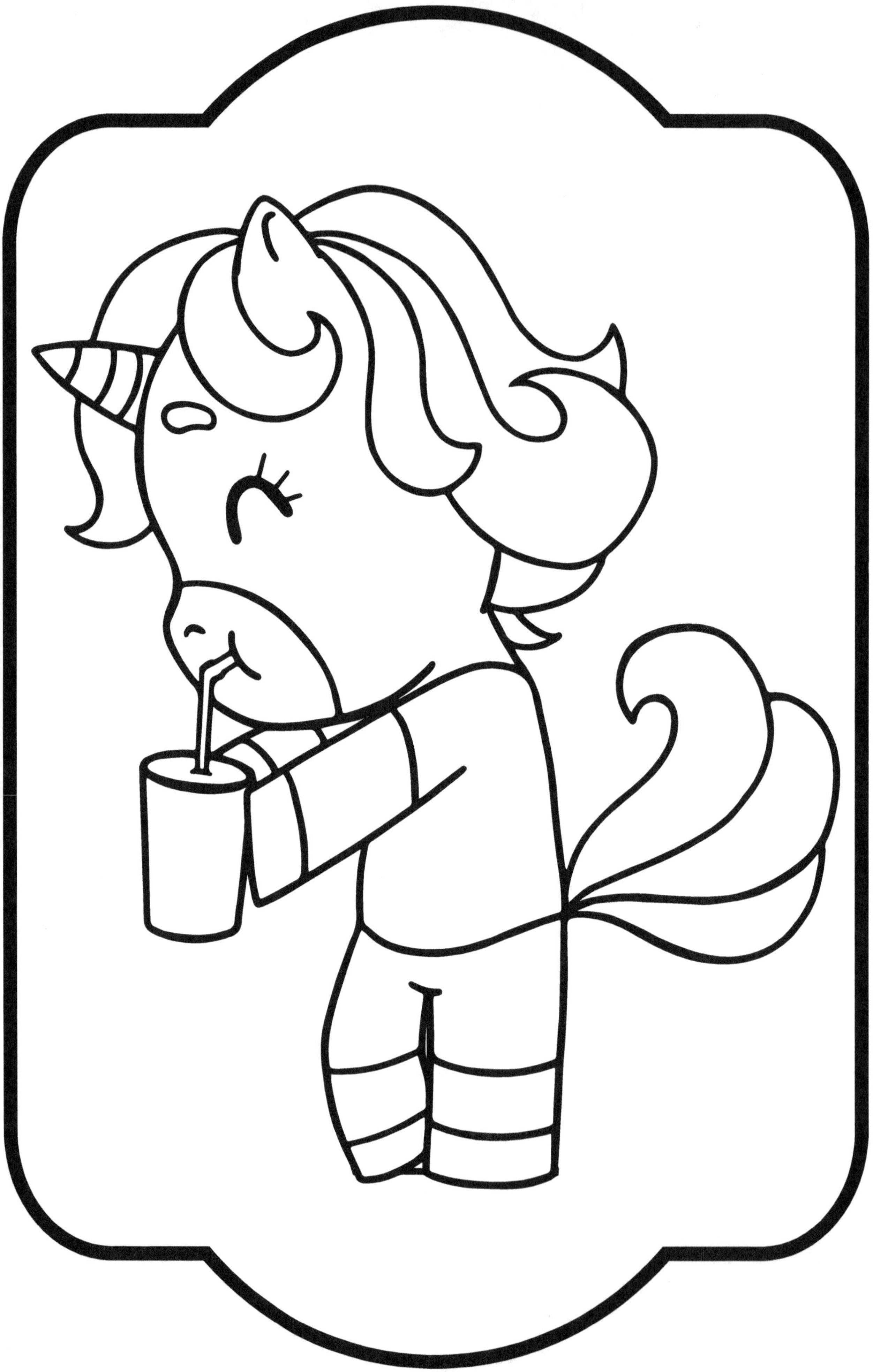

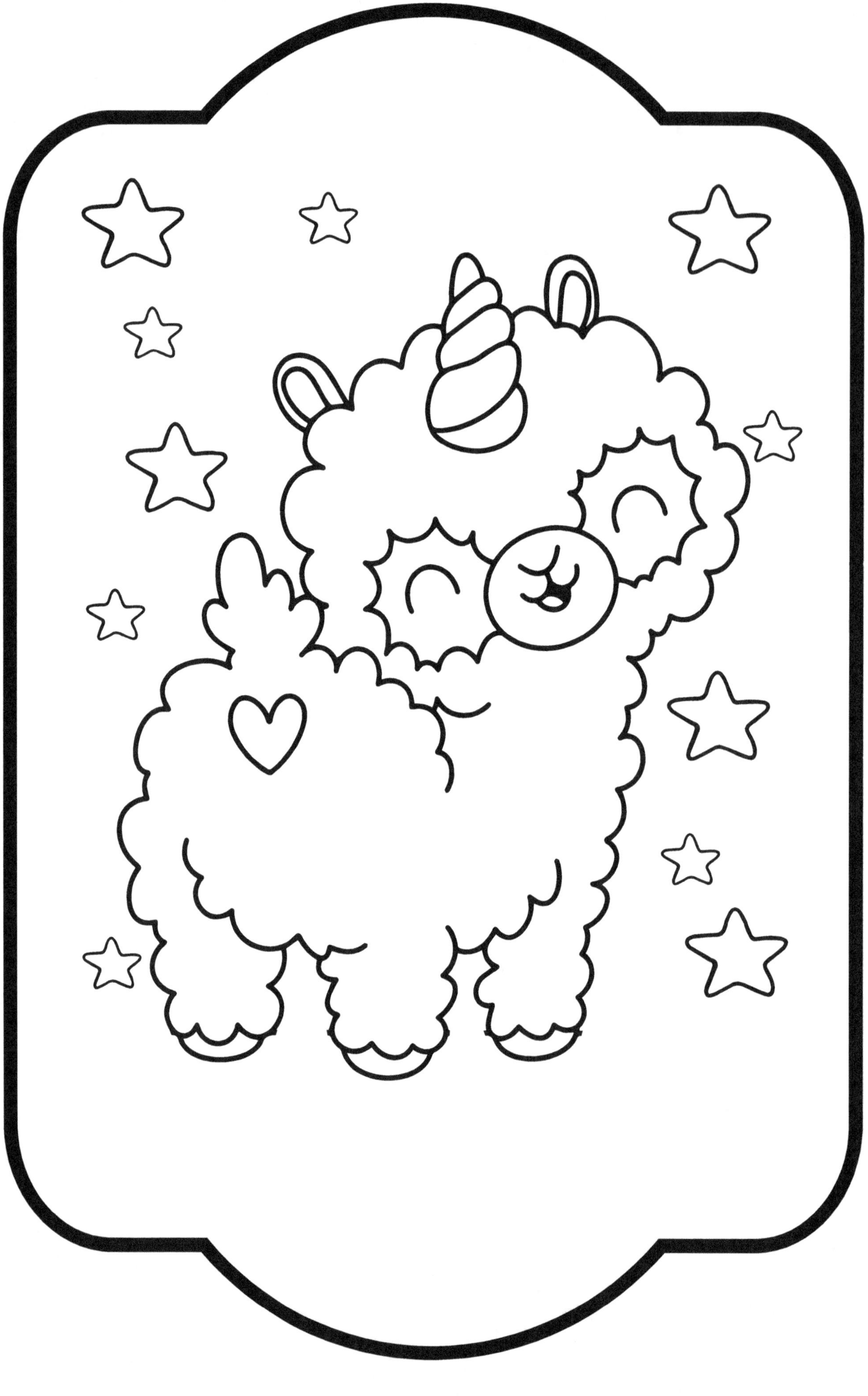

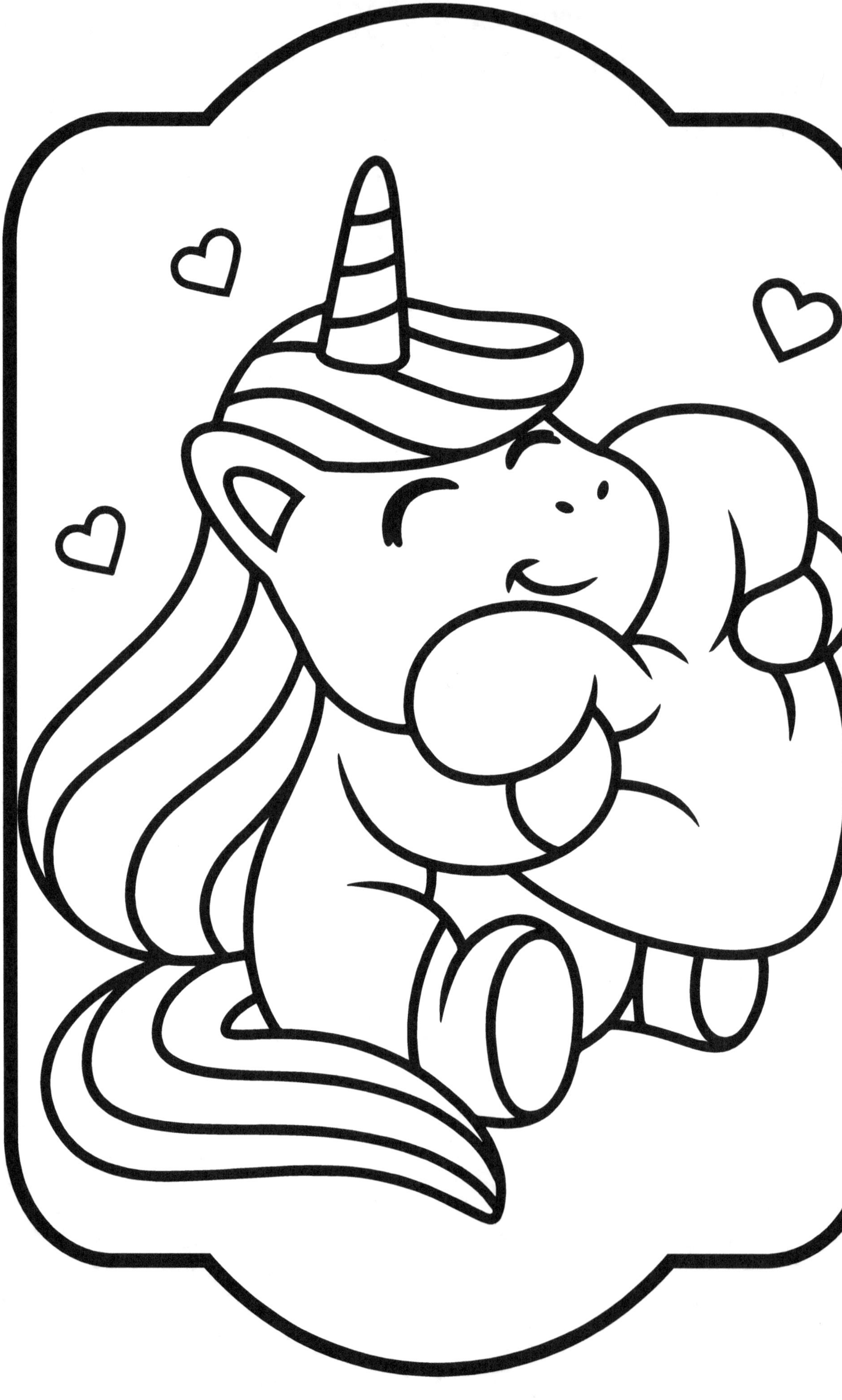

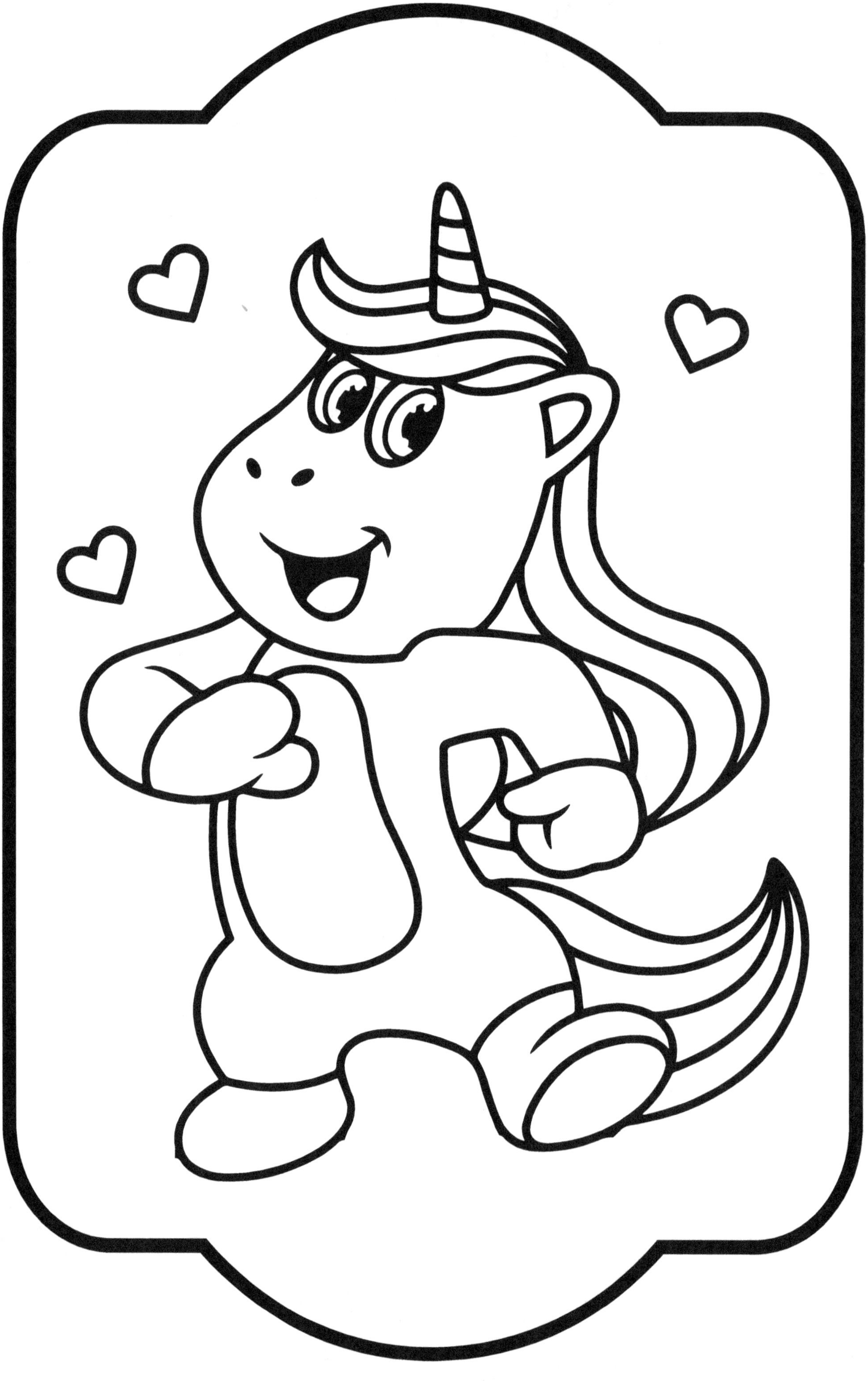

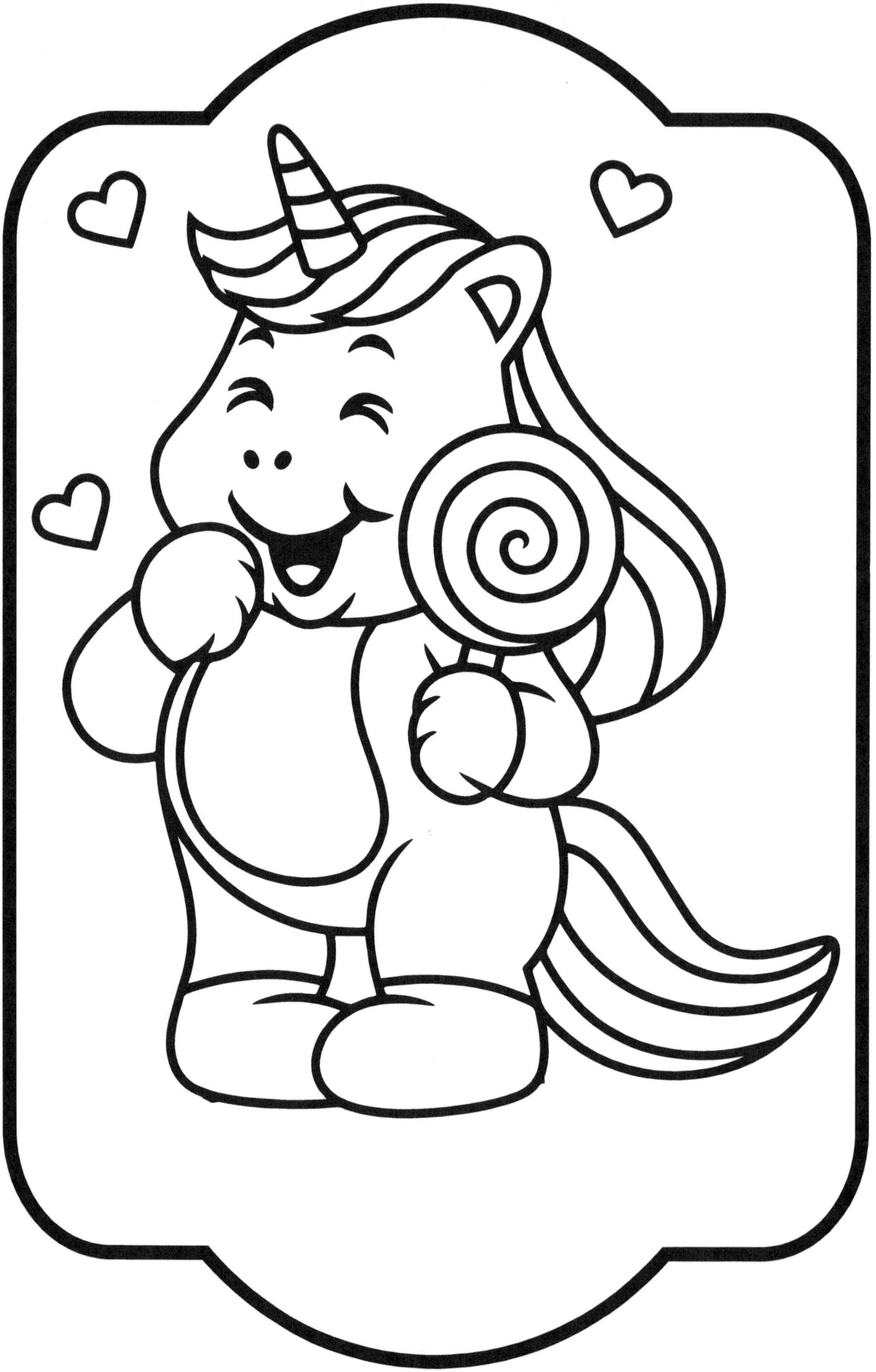

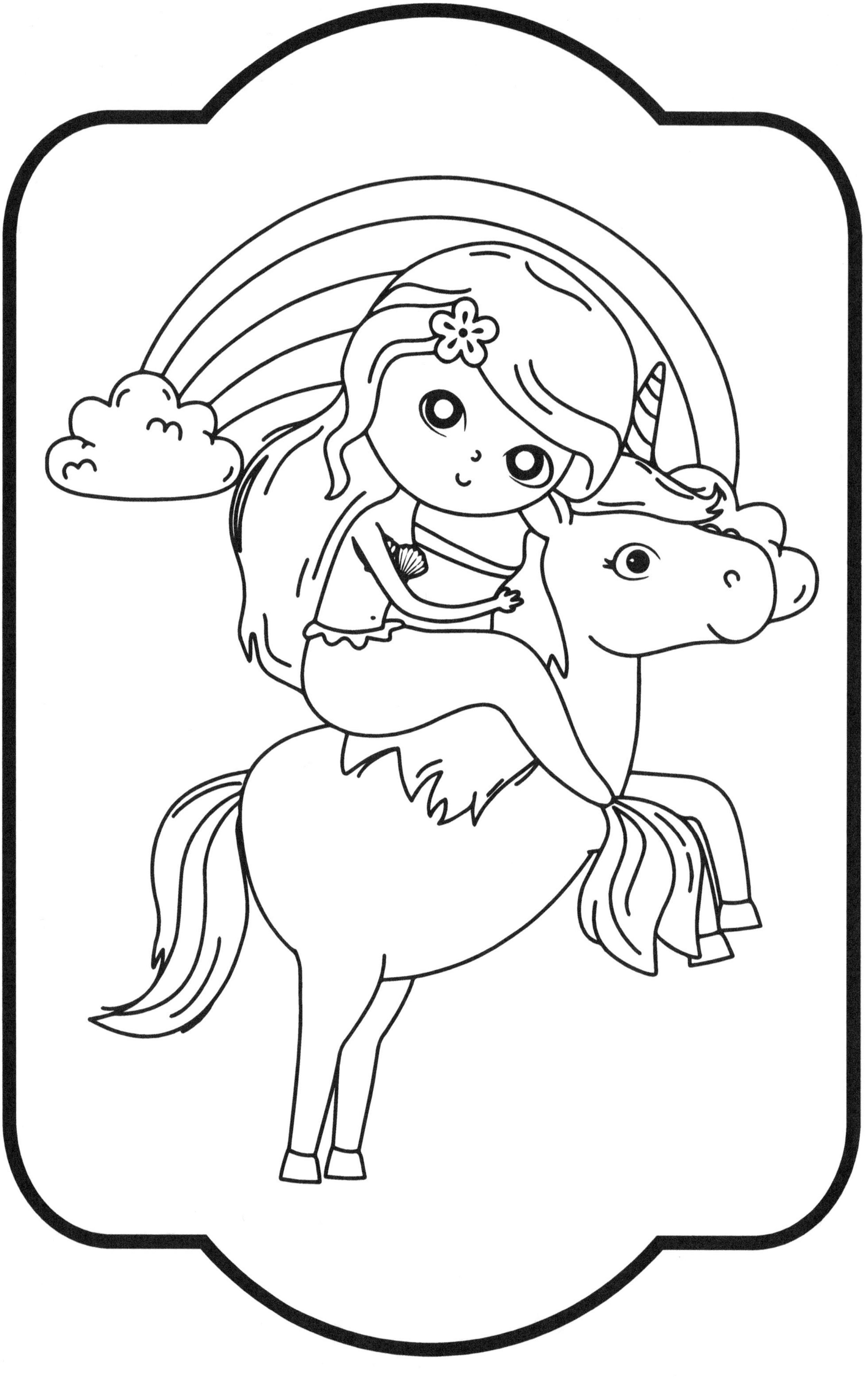

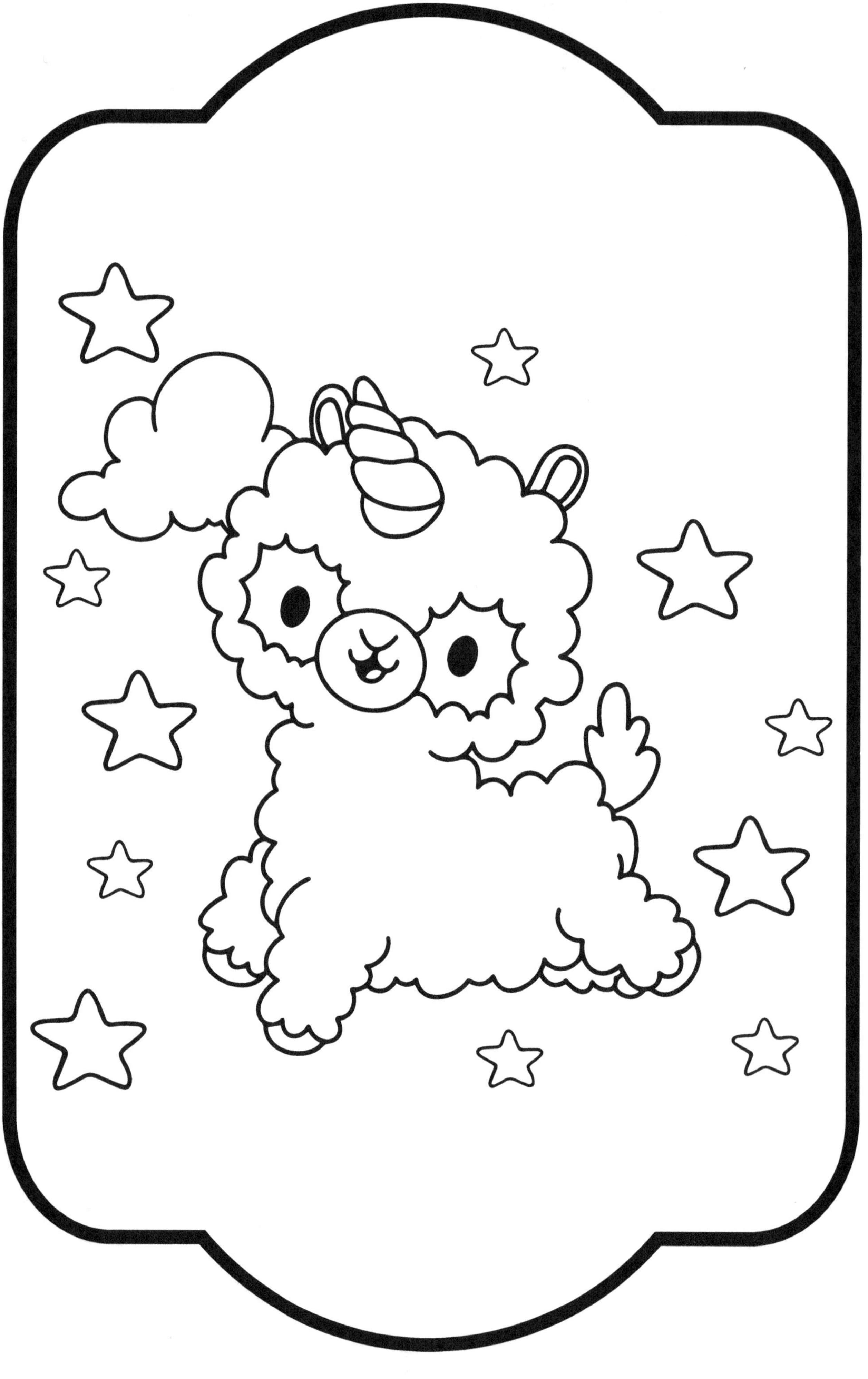

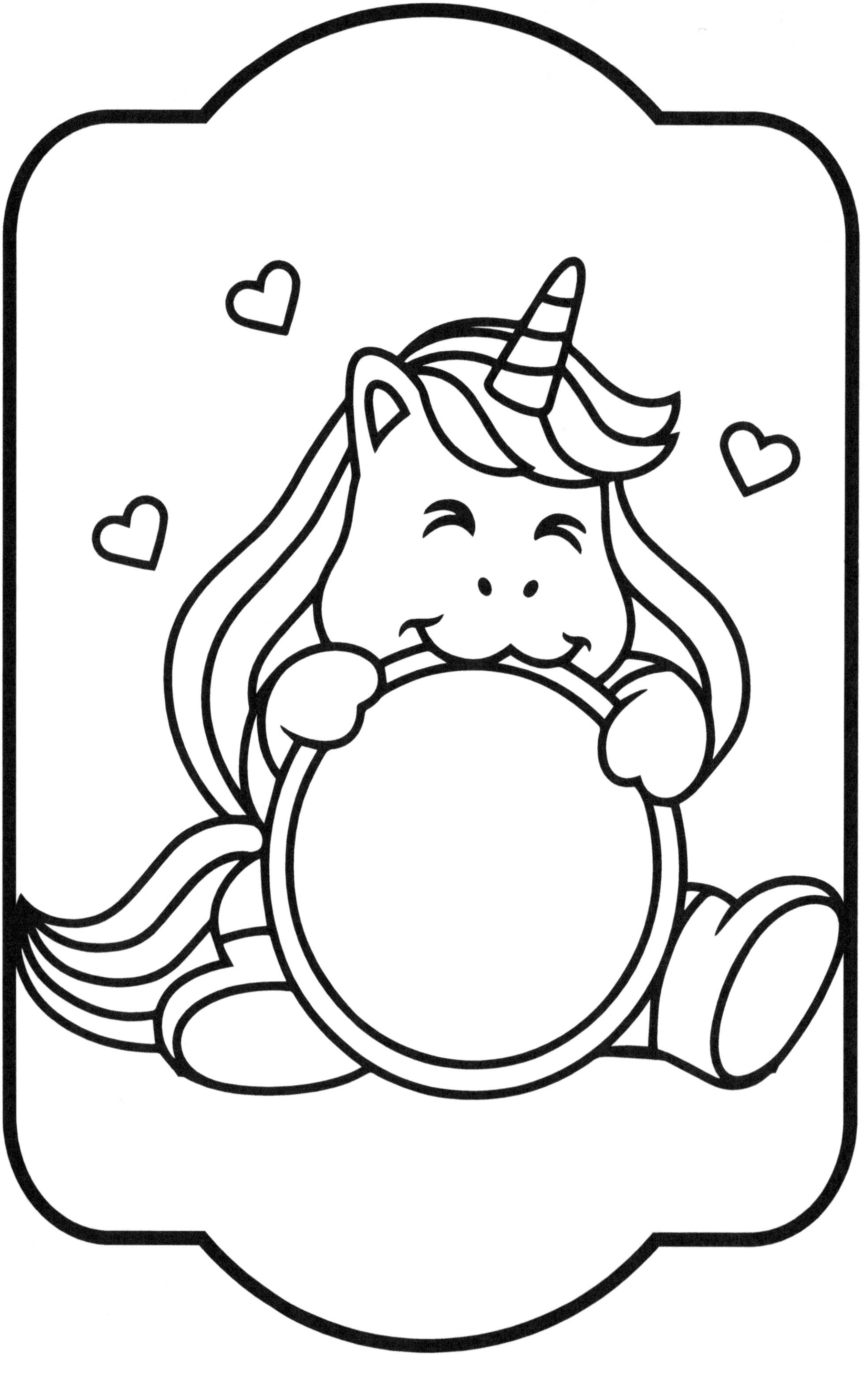

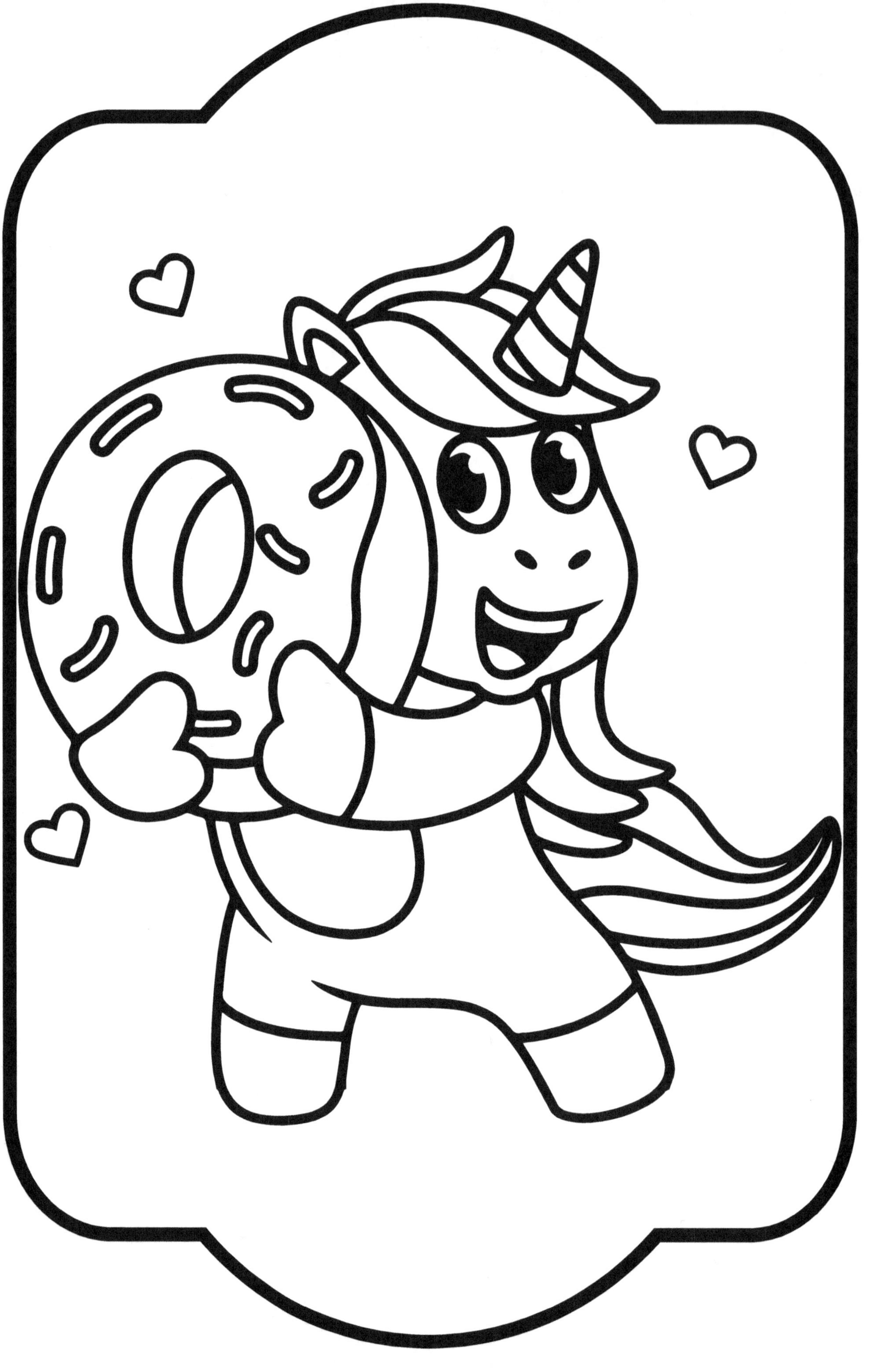

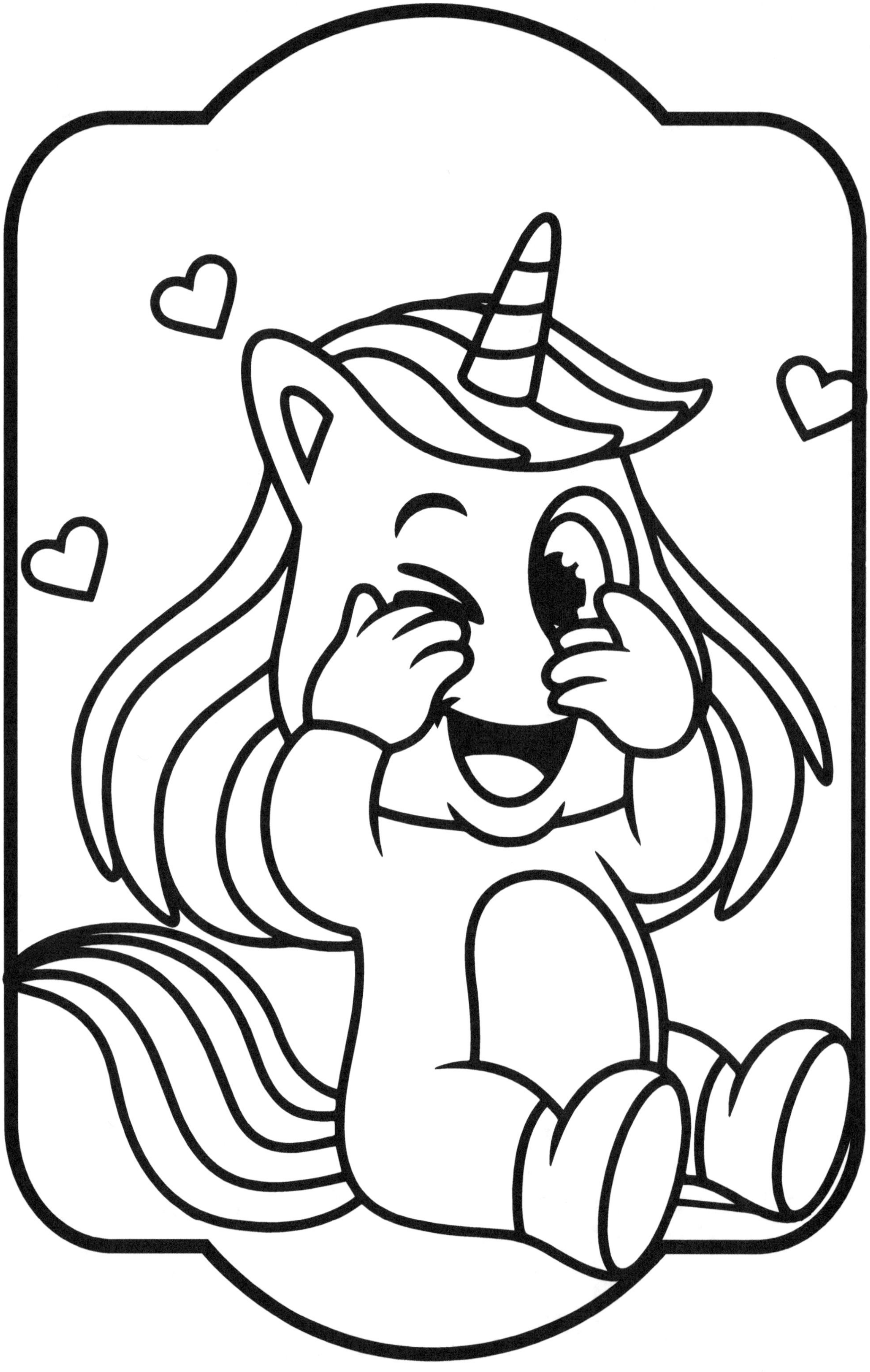

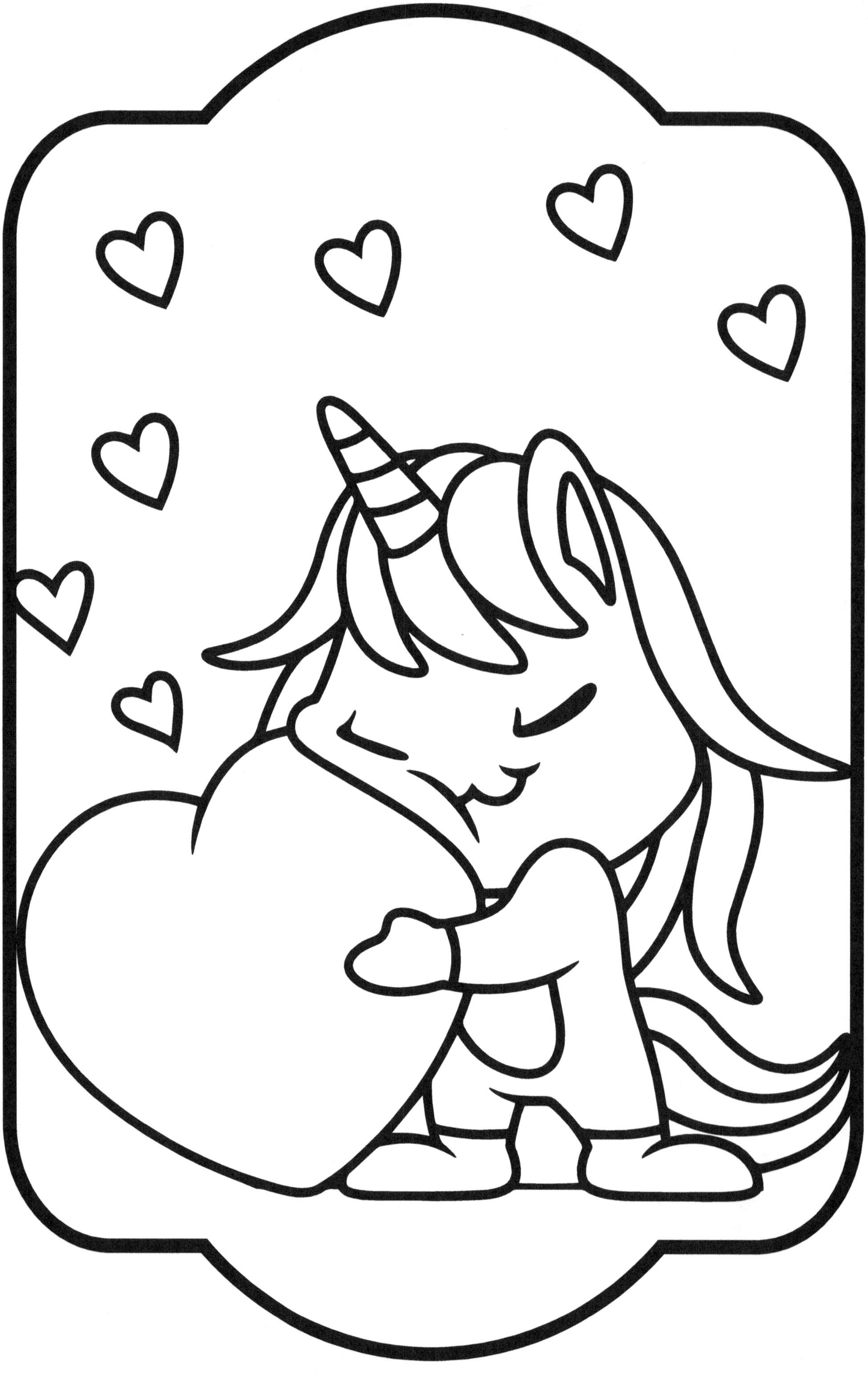

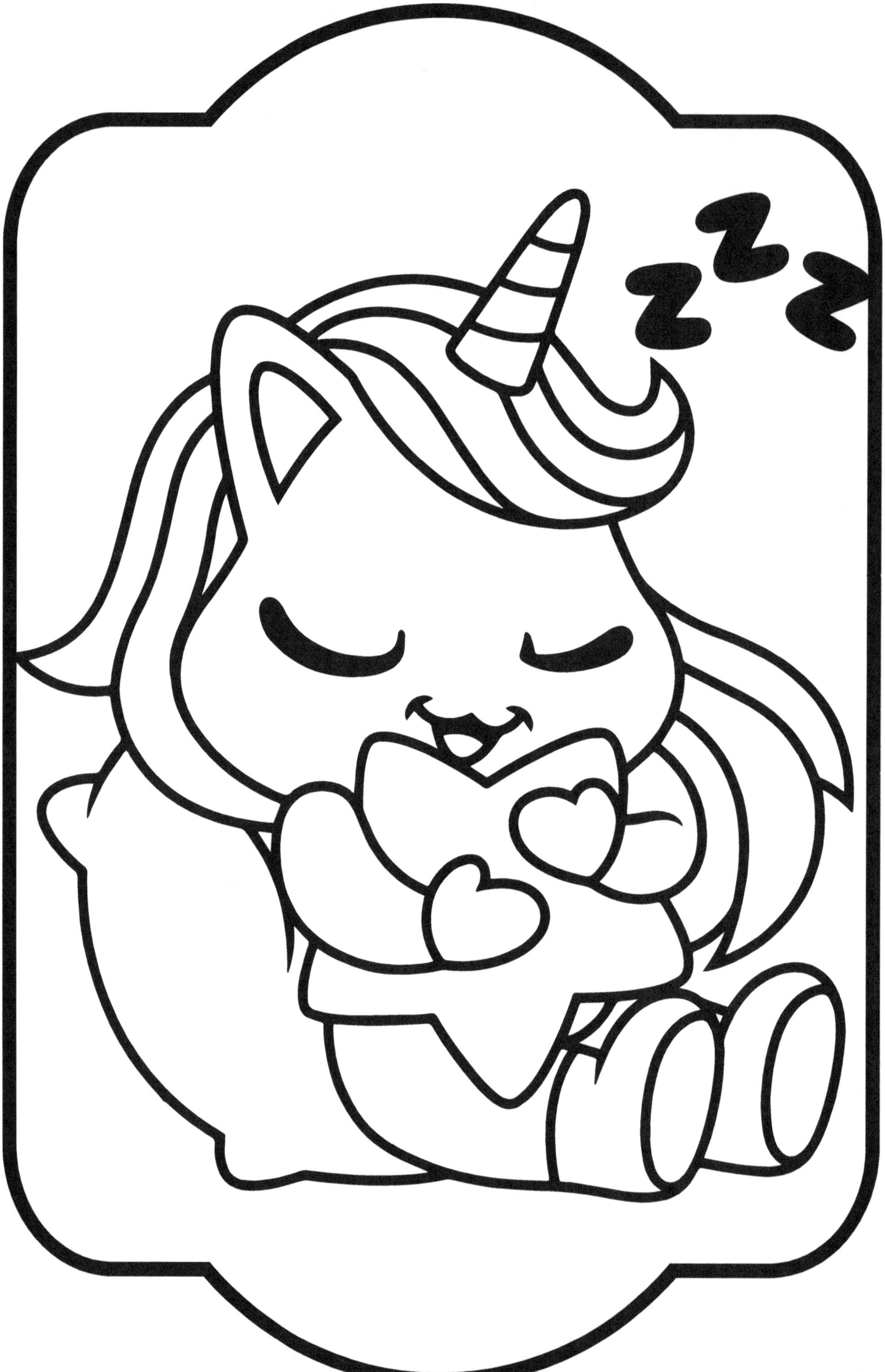
ZZZ

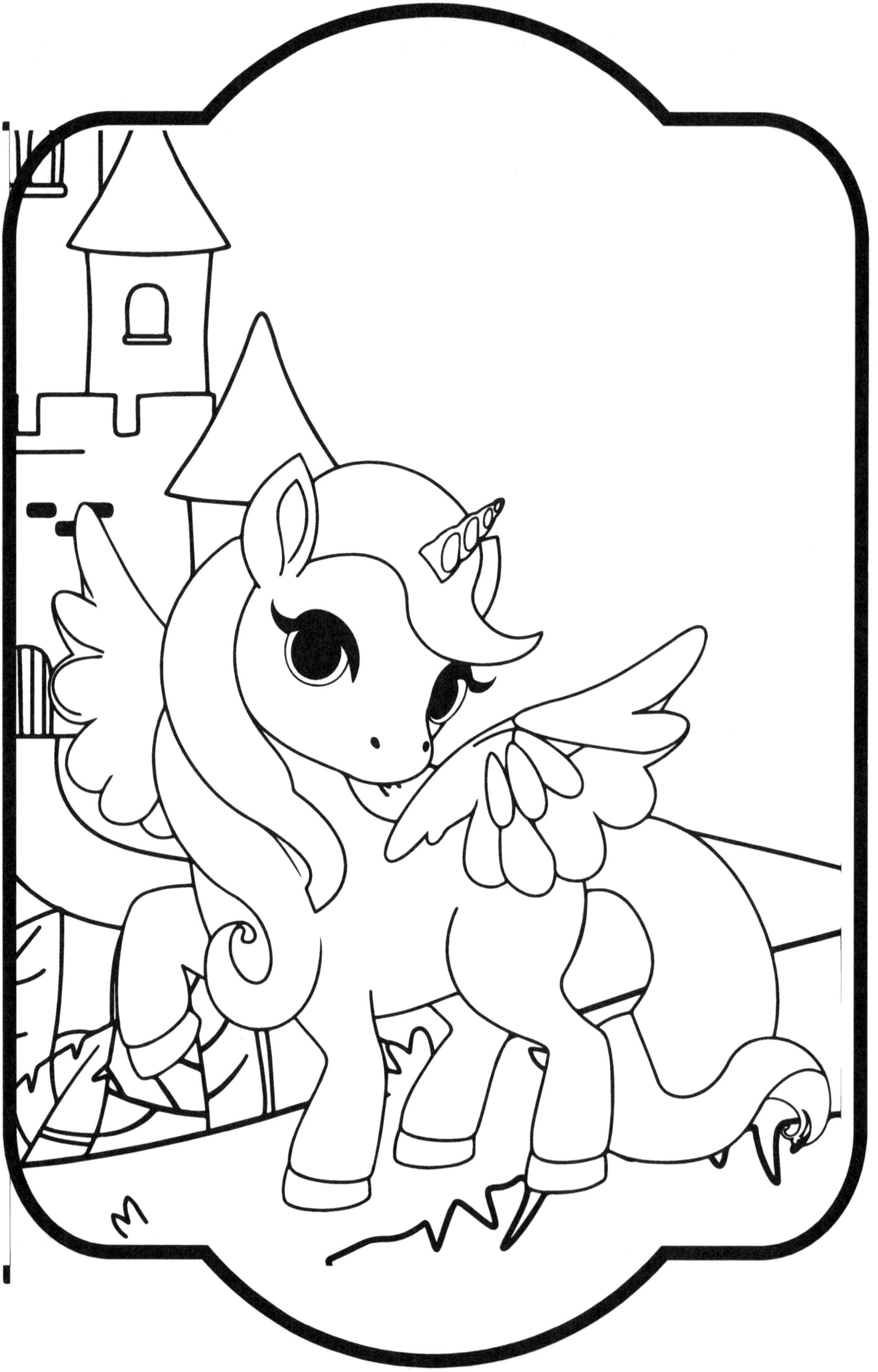

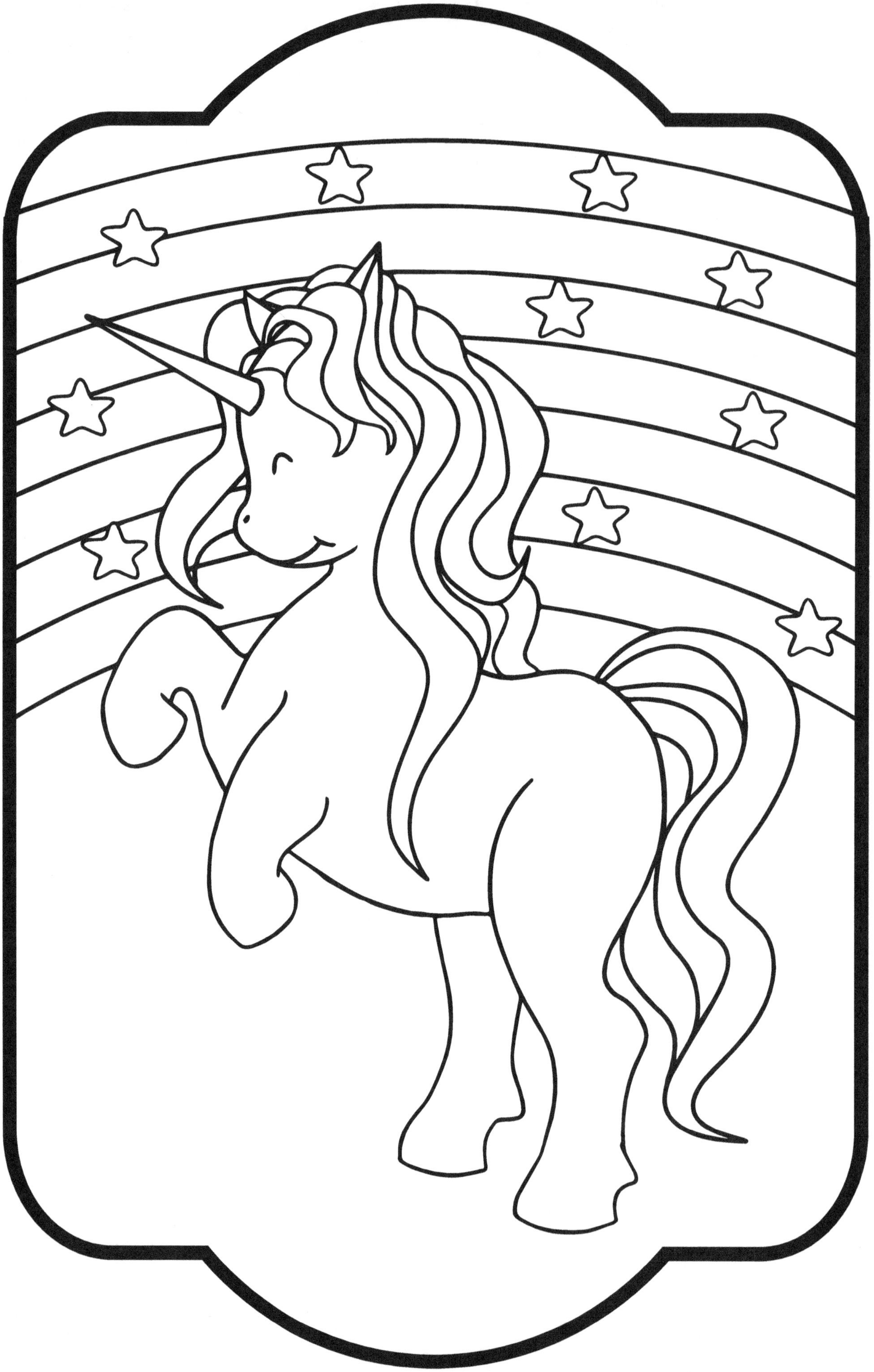

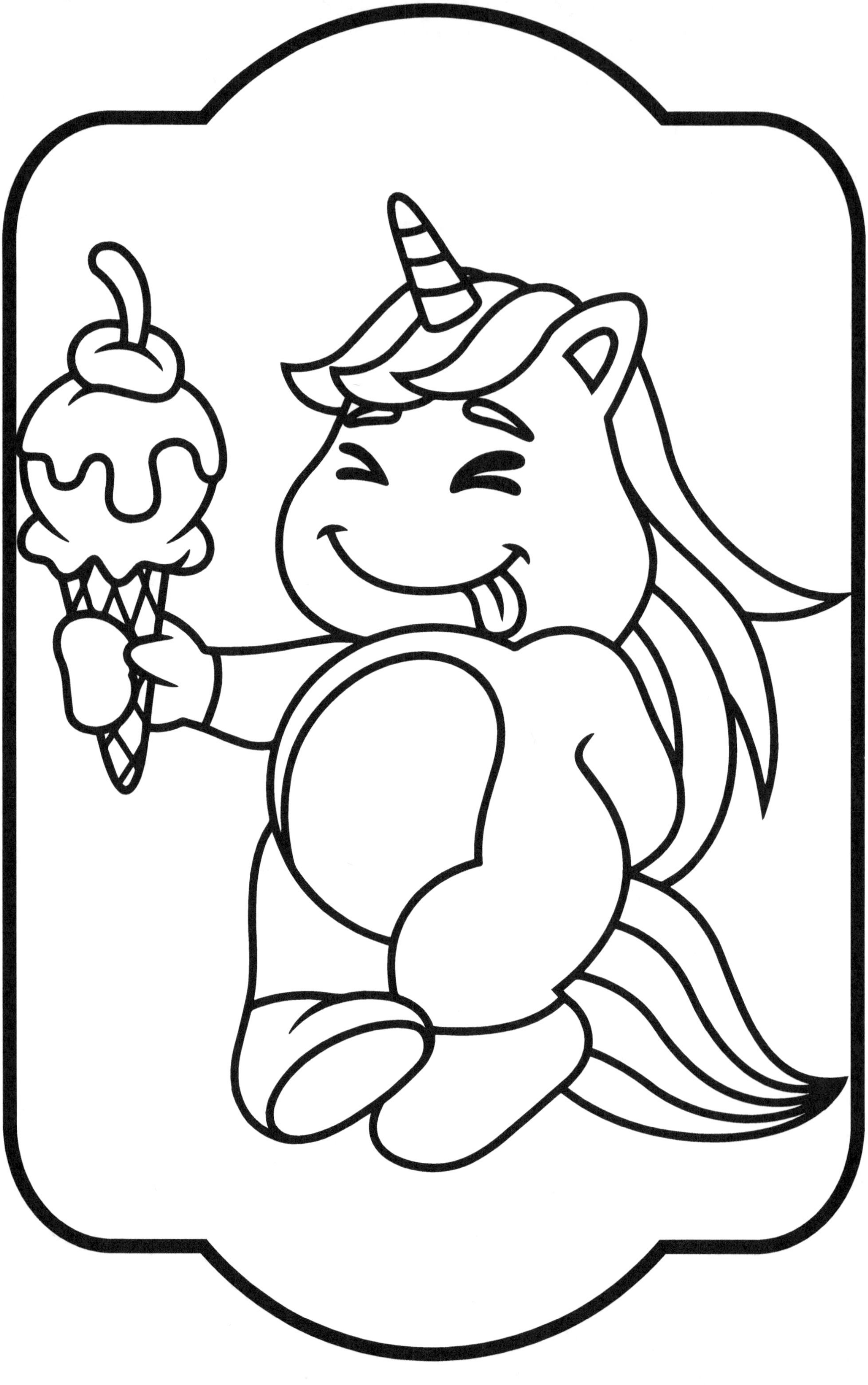

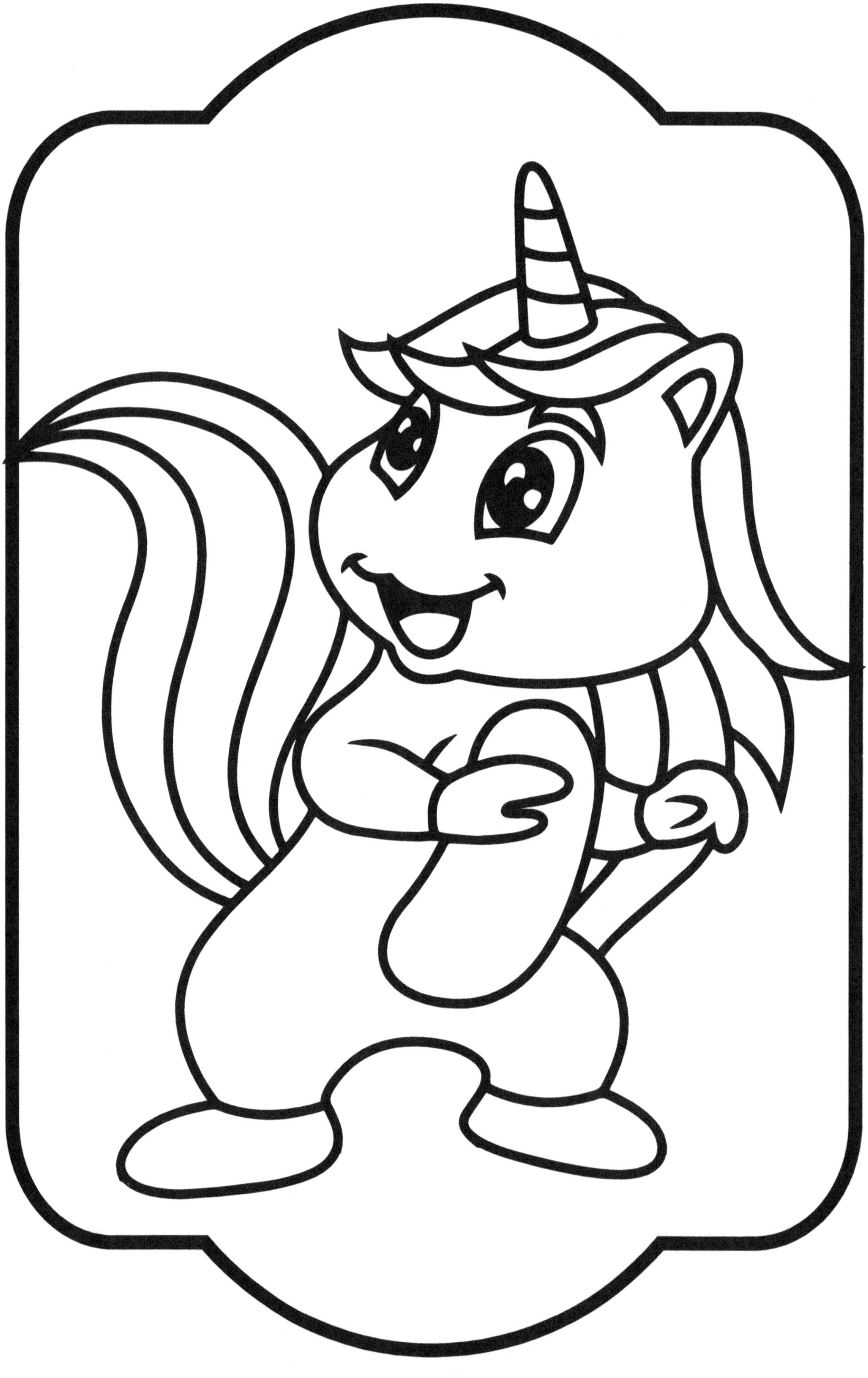

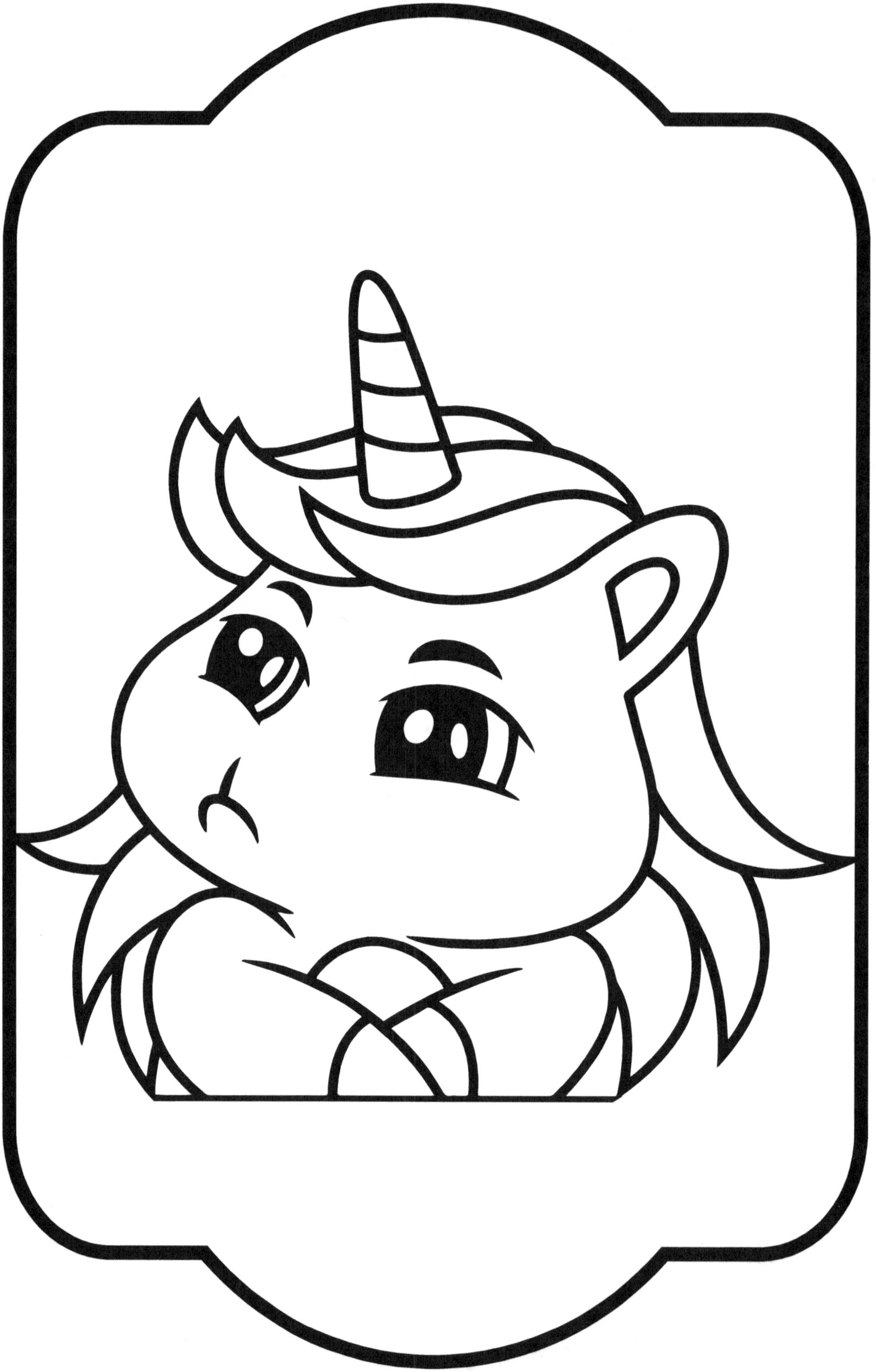

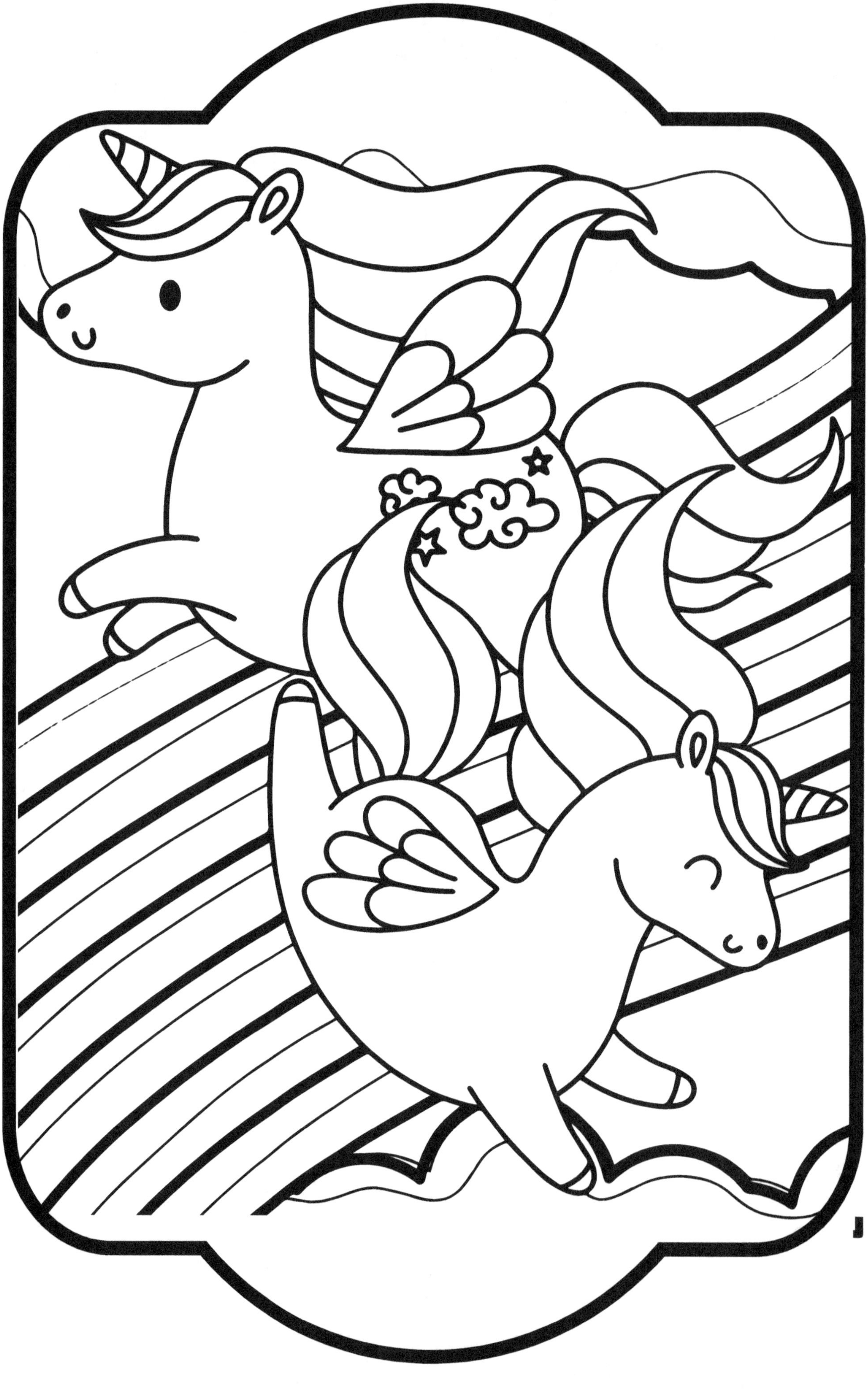

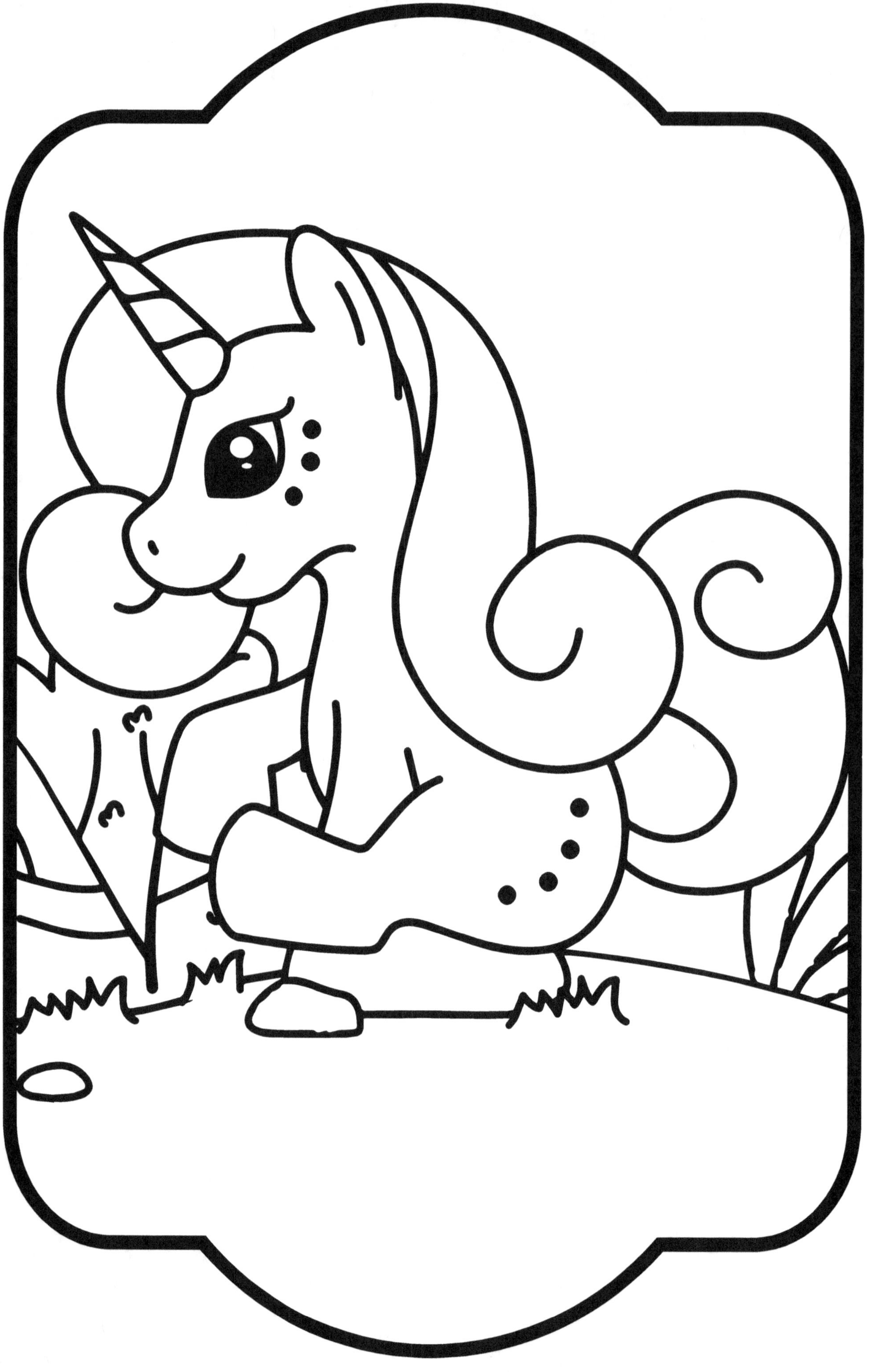

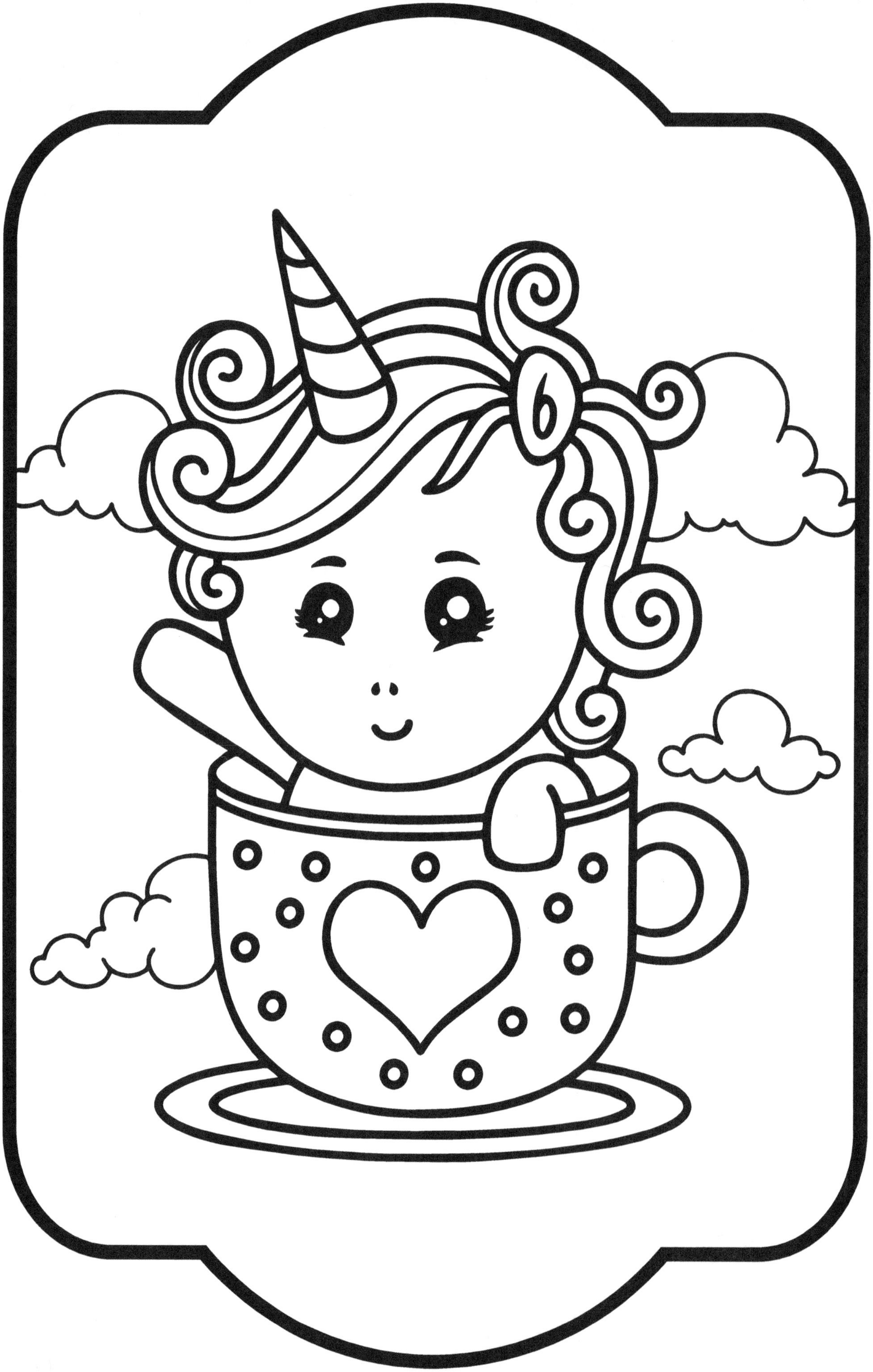

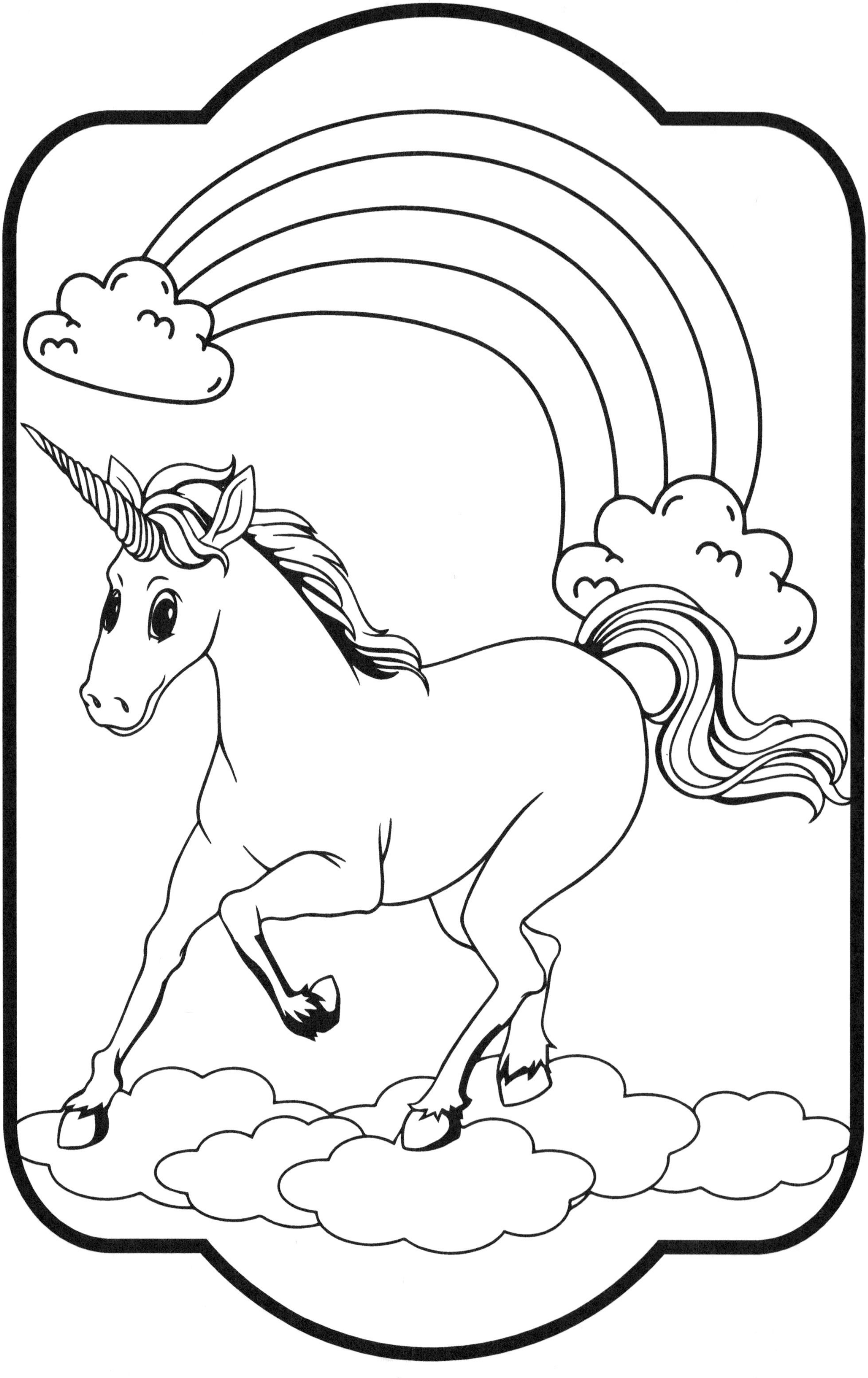

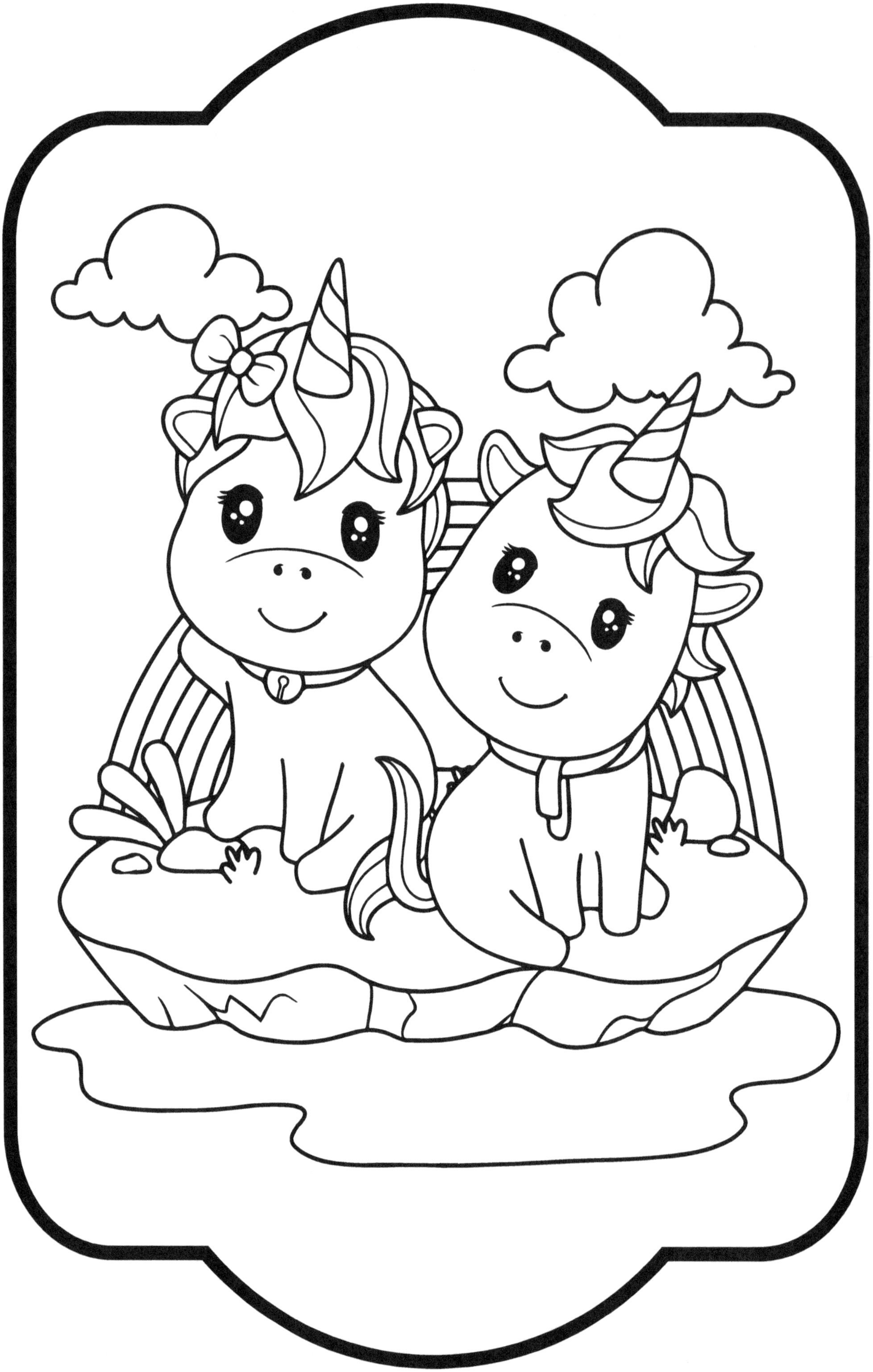

www.ingramcontent.com/pod-product-compliance
Lightning Source LLC
Chambersburg PA
CBHW081418220526
45467CB00009B/2727
* 9 7 9 8 7 2 8 3 9 7 4 8 9 *